THE BEST FRIENDS

Guide to Spectacular Sleepovers

SCHOLASTIC INC.

New York   Toronto   London   Auckland   Sydney
Mexico City   New Delhi   Hong Kong   Buenos Aires

ISBN 0-439-68945-7

Text copyright © 2003 by Gill Sutherland
Illustrations copyright © 2003 by Kirstie Aitken

12 11 10 9 8 7 6 5 4 3   5 6 7 8 9/0

Printed in the U.S.A.   40

First printing, November 2004

Contents

 ★ Want to Be Friends? ★

Hi! I'm Molly White, aka The Author, and am I pleased to meet you! Just so you know, I'm a diplomatic Libra, share my mom and dad with my incredibly annoying twin bro Billy, and live in a sort of urban sprawl we'll call Dullsville. Naturally, I'm gorgeous to behold and something of a genius. (OK, really I'm a little short, sometimes get zits, have spiky hair that no amount of conditioner will tame into a glossy sheen, and my teachers claim I'm "easily distracted" and "lazy.") I like long words, chocolate, art, saving the planet, cheese puffs, poems, most music, wise people, and, of course, sleepover parties! I do *not* like pollution or broccoli.

But that's enough about me. I've heard that you're here for fabulous tips and ideas about how to put on the best sleepover EVER. Well, you've definitely come to the right place, because me and the gang are here to help. ... So come on — it's time to meet your new Best Friends!

Flower

AKA: Flower Spirit Delaney (hello, hippie parents!)

Star sign: Dreamy Pisces

Likes: "Animals, wildlife, and my mom teaching me about feng shui and other new-age stuff."

Dislikes: "Nothing. I like *everything*!"

Sleepovers held: "A couple — for my last one, I did a love theme for Valentine's Day — with heart-shaped pizza and mushy videos. Me and the Friends also made tons of glittery Valentine cards and sent them out anonymously at school!"

Missy

AKA: Nora Baxter (don't call her that, though, she gets annoyed...)

Star sign: Crabby Cancer

Likes: "I'm heavily into R&B and jazz, and I love urban clothes. Plus, you'll never see me without my cell!"

Dislikes: "Being without my phone — like in class — and being without my pals."

Sleepovers held: "People drop in at my place all the time... at a guess, like, ten a year."

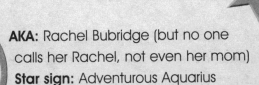

Bubble

AKA: Rachel Bubridge (but no one calls her Rachel, not even her mom)

Star sign: Adventurous Aquarius

Likes: "Mega-loud rock music, running, having a laugh with my friends, playing pranks, world travel, and FOOOOD (lots of it)!!!"

Dislikes: "Mean people. Dresses. Oh, and being tall and gangly."

Sleepovers held: "I'm what you'd call a very experienced, uhm, guest — it's hassle-free, so you can just enjoy yourself!"

Princess

AKA: Pandora Moxbury (now does that sound classy, or does that sound classy?)

Star sign: Sophisticated Aries

Likes: "I adore clothes, shopping, fashion magazines, and interior design."

Dislikes: "Bad-hair days and having no money to spend."

Sleepovers held: "Tons! I love being the hostess with the mostest — whether it's a birthday, Halloween, New Year, or because it's the weekend — any excuse will do!"

Impressed so far? I hope so, because together we Best Friends have heaps of incredible ideas, awesome advice, and terrific tips to make sure you put on the Best Sleepover in the World! Stick with us and you'll find out how to:

★ Win your parents over with our surefire techniques!
★ Make perfect painless plans for a perfect party!
★ Ease your worries with the coolest problem page in the cosmos!

What's more, you can do our quiz to find out what sort of sleepover girl YOU are. And, as you're officially now our New Best Friend, we offer the following guarantee of true friendship:

The Best Friends' pledge

1. To be on hand with our expert advice 24/7, sleeping by your side if necessary.

★

2. To never give up on you — even if you completely ignore our advice.

★

3. To ~~never~~ hardly ever laugh at your mistakes, off-the-wall fads, and truly crazy ideas.

★

4. Basically, you have our undying love, loyalty blah de blah de blah, and can borrow any of our things, any time... for eternity!

OK, onward! — your sleepover's not going to organize itself, Friend. So, let's get down to some serious preparation....

Getting Started

So, you've decided to host a sleepover — congratulations! You are in for a fantastic time! OK, let's start with the most basic question in the world: WHAT IS A SLEEPOVER? Princess, O Queen of Sleepovers, perhaps you can answer that one?

"Easy. A sleepover is when you have a group of friends over to stay the night. You do stuff like play games, watch videos, munch on yummy snacks, and have giggle attacks when you should be sleeping. It can also be called a 'slumber party' or 'pajama party.'**"**

"But what if our new Friend has the kind of parents who just, like, say 'No way' to her having a sleepover?**"**

Hmm, that's a tough one, Bubs, but there are ways around it. . . .

Winning The Parents' Permission

There are many ways to get The Parents to let you have a sleepover party. Let's run through the different approaches to "Parent Persuasion," as we Best Friends like to call it.

Beg: Hands clasped, down on bended knee, whiny voice: "Oh, puh-leeeeasssse" etc.

Tantrum: Foot stomping, bedroom door slamming...and general bratlike behavior until they "surrender."

Bully/bribe: Said with a pouty voice: "If you don't let me, I don't see how I can possibly concentrate on my schoolwork." Similarly: "I promise I'll work double-hard at school."

Nag relentlessly: Like begging, except it's 24 hours a day.

Flatter: "You know I really think you're the best parents a girl could have" etc.

Cry: Silent, dignified dewdrops dabbed gracefully away, or great snotty howls — you decide.

Sulk: Dark looks and absolutely zero speech.

The classic: To Dad: "But Mom said I could," and vice versa. Or: "But you promised last year!"

The birthday special: Wailed with real injustice: "But it's MY BIRTHDAY!!!"

Best Friends TOP TIP

Whether you try these approaches on your mom or dad, or both together, what you are looking for is a crack in their armor — a sign that they might be weakening. Once you spot this — go for it big-time!

❝If I really want something, I text-message mom's cell with ☺ or ☹ faces, depending on whether she says yes or no.**❞**

If the persuasion campaign fails you, and you don't have a cell phone like our Missy, we Best Friends suggest a formal written letter, like this:

Dear Mr. & Mrs. _____ (your last name here),

Please let your loving daughter _____ (your name here) have ____ (number of guests here) friends to stay for a sleepover on the night of _____ (date here). If you do, we hereby promise that we will tidy up after ourselves, keep the noise down, and turn you into some sort of legend of cool parentdom across the playgrounds of this great land of ours.

Sincerely,
(potential sleepover guests and hostess sign here)

"And if they STILL won't give in, what's a girl to do?**"**

There's only one desperate option remaining, I'm afraid: the "I'm really a very sensible young lady" approach. This is how it's done: Ask your parents to sit down for a few minutes to talk about your proposed sleepover, then show them the following tips for parents. Finally, offer to discuss in a CALM and MATURE way the worries they may still have about your proposed sleepover.

"A bit of compromise will get you a long way, girl!**"**

Five parental rules for stress-free sleepovers

1 Make sure the girls have lots of energetic activities planned — it keeps them out of trouble and tires them out for bedtime.

2 Provide a few healthy snacks for them to eat with the junk food to prevent sickness and hyperactivity.

3 Establish the rules in a very brief pre-party "chat" — no fighting, crank phone calls, mean tricks, leaving the house, or unsupervised cooking. And set a bedtime.

4 Suggest they watch an hour or so of videos before bedtime. (They'll soon be nodding off.)

5 Avoid embarrassing your beloved daughter, by staying out of the way (except when needed).

So have you persuaded your mom and dad? Hurray! (If not, turn to the Best Friends' problem solver on page 98, for further advice.) That means you're ready for the next step on the road to sleepover success. Now you can start making plans — things are about to get really exciting!

Molly has a quiet word about M-O-N-E-Y

Call me Ms. Fusspants, but before you get carried away ordering a gallon of the finest cookieslurp-doublefudge-almond-nugget ice cream delivered on matching white ponies for each of your fabulous guests, let's think about this: How much money can you spend? You don't need a lot of money to make your party fun, but working out a budget will help you make the most of what you *do* have.

We want this to be a relaxing, enjoyable day (and night!), and planning ahead is the key. A good place to start is by making lots of lists.

The how-to-do-a-sleepover-list list!

1 Write down EVERYTHING you need for your sleepover (people, invites, food, games, videos, DVDs, etc.).

2 Check-off each thing as it is figured out...

3 ...or add "*X*" next to difficult-to-plan things.

4 Write down costs of *everything*, revising as you go.

5 Get a clipboard if you want to look like a pro.

6 Make sure you've sorted out your "*X*" items by the morning of the sleepover.

7 Do *not* still be clutching this precious list as your friends arrive (so not cool).

❀ Flower's sleepover list ❀

Theme: Valentine's Day
Guest list: Molly, Missy, Princess, Bubble, and me!
Date: Feb. 12 (Held on Saturday so we can make Valentine cards
and give them out at school on Monday)
Start time: 7 pm **Finishing:** 11 am the next morning!

Thing!

Invitations:
Pink card for heart-shaped invites . . . .
Glitter pen . . . .
Stamps . . . .

Room arrangements & decorations:
Figure out where everyone is to sleep, plus blankets, pillows, etc. . . . .
Balloons and streamers . . . .

Tidy up very messy bedroom!!! . . . .
Chocolate hearts for Best Friends — to let them know how much I looove them! . . . . . .

Food:
Pizza (including toppings and dough) . . . .
Heart-shaped pan (for pizza) . . . .
Pretzels and chips, soft drinks, and stuff for sundaes . . . .
Mountains of melon and fruit chunks for breakfast . . . .

Entertainment:
Two mushy love-story videos . . . .
Valentine card-making material (including envelopes,
cards, heart stickers, and stamps) . . . .

Posters and old lipstick for kissy-kissy poster game (see page 70) . . . .

Miscellaneous:
Make sure best PJs are clean . . . .
Check toothpaste and toilet paper levels! . . . .

> **"** Okay, here's my Valentine's Day sleepover superplan. Don't forget to fill in the cost of things, and jot down any ideas you have along the way! **"**

Action ★	Progress ✓ done ✗ to do	Cost
Make cards and send out two weeks before		
Already got		
Buy from P.O.		
Mom to do week before the party		
Dad to dig out leftover ones from New Year's Eve as soon as he "finds time" – Put up on morning of party		
2 days before		
Leave under each Friend's pillow before bedtime — aw!		
Buy ingredients day before — Set up kitchen by 5:30 pm		
Dig out from cupboard day before		
Buy day before		
Dad or Mom buy fresh on day of party and prep for morning after		
Mom renting on the morning of party		
Buy weekend before — Lay out equipment on desk in my room on day of sleepover		
Save magazines from last month — Go through three days before selecting potential smooch victims — Beg Mom for old lipsticks		
Three days before		
Day before		

"Wow! That's way impressive, Flower! No wonder we all had such a fab time that night!**"**

Hold your galloping horses, though, Friends! Before you begin making your superplan, there are some MAJOR decisions you've got to make first. I call them the four Ws, and they are the stars of our next chapter.

The Four Ws: When, What, Where, and Who

❝Ooh, these sound a little scary!**❞**

Not at all, Bubble. These four lovely little words are our pals, because once you've made the big decisions like...

when to have your sleepover

where you're going to sleep

what kind of theme you want your evening to have

who to invite

...everything will fall magically into place! Honest!

When to do your sleepover

You may be tempted to hold your sleepover on a week night if it's for something special like a birthday. This is OK if it's during school vacations, but otherwise it's best to hold it on a Saturday night.

❝Uhm, why?**❞**

66Because, Flower, you'll be too pooped from partying all night for school the next day, and on Fridays you'll be too pooped from school to party all night! So it's gotta be a Saturday.... And, in my experience, the best sleepovers follow a rough timetable, like this... **99**

Princess's sample sleepover schedule

6 pm	Guests arrive – chat, hang out, get changed into pajamas
7 pm	Pizza-eating
7:30 pm	Making and munching of gooey ice cream sundaes
8 pm	Games and karaoke
9:30 pm	Videos and popcorn
11 pm	Tooth-brushing and bed
All night	Giggling, jokes, scary storytelling, etc.
10 am	Fruit –filled breakfast
10:30 am	Get dressed
11 am	Watch video we made during karaoke the night before
11:30–12 pm	Guests leave (sob!)

Way to go, Princess. That sounds like the **when** is figured out. Now we've got to think about **where** your guests are going to sleep!

66What sleep? I wanna parteeee all night!**99**

66That's why we always call your sleepovers 'Missy's nosleepovers,' you wild and crazy girl!**99**

(Said in sensible Author's voice . . .) Thinking about where you and your friends are going to sleep will give you a realistic idea of how many you can invite. But it doesn't have to be a case of "two in my bed and two in sleeping bags" — use your imagination to make the most of the space available. You may also want to start thinking about **what** kind of theme you want your sleepover to have. Come on, let's see what the Best Friends might do. . . .

Flower's exotic emporium

❝I think I must have been a belly dancer in a previous life because I'd love to spend the night in one of those luxury Bedouin tents! Anyway, this is my cheapo version!**❞**

Theme: Hippie meets Eastern desert chic

Good for: small bedrooms

Approx number of guests: four

1 See if your parents will let you clear as much furniture (including your bed) out of your room as possible.

2 Cover the floor with cushions or blankets with sheets spread on top.

3 Ask Mom or Dad to change all the lightbulbs in your room to colored ones — creating a softer light and more intimate feel.

4 Spray sandalwood perfume (or similar spicy scent) around for some, ahem, "exotic smells of the East."

5 Finally, for a truly magical touch, drape string lights around the room. Ta-daa! A cozy tiny den fit for Arabian princesses!

Bubble's big hee-haw ✦✦ 🌙

❝Camping is great fun – but if cloudy skies and parents mean that's a no-no, then use your imagination and take a walk on the Wild-West side with me!❞

Theme: Cowgirls go camping

Good for: bigger bedrooms

Approx number of guests: six

1 Make a night sky by getting a load of thin cardboard (old greeting cards or cereal boxes will do) and cutting out tons of different-sized stars and moon crescents.

2 Paint your shapes with glow-in-the-dark paint — leaving the first side to dry before flipping each shape over and doing the second side.

3 Make a hole in the top of each shape with a hole punch — or, if you don't have one, you can do this:

Place your shape on a magazine or thick newspaper on top of a stable surface (kitchen counter, etc.) and carefully twist the point of a pair of scissors to create a small hole. Note the use of the word *carefully* there!

4 Put a piece of thread — about 32 inches (80 cm) or so in length — through a shape's hole. Pull the thread through until the shape's hole is at the thread's halfway mark. Hold the two ends of thread together and tie in a knot — so you now have a loop of thread attached to this shape. Repeat with the rest of the shapes.

5 Now hang them from the ceiling, with securely fixed thumbtacks or Sticky Tac.

6 Lay out your guests' sleeping bags in a circle.

7 For a fabulous pretend campfire, get the string lights out and place them in a big heap in the center of the circle. Turn out all the lights except your "campfire," and admire the twinkling night sky above!

8 Continue your Wild West theme by serving nachos, hot dogs, and baked beans for munchies.

Missy's movie magic

66 Glam up, then veg out — everyone will love it! 99

Theme: Glamorous video-thon

Good for: living rooms

Approx number of guests: eight

1 Rent two or three of the latest video/DVD releases — go for a mix like a funny, a sad, and an action or a thriller (but not, like, freaky-nightmare scary).

2 Paint sheets of newspaper red, then lay them down in a "carpet" leading up to your front door, fixing it down with masking tape or with small rocks from the outdoors (be sure you wash them off before you bring them into the house!).

3 Decorate the walls of your "movie theater" with posters of Hollywood heartthrobs you've saved from old magazines — use Sticky Tac to avoid marking the walls.

4 Set up your guests' sleeping positions around the TV so everyone gets a good view.

5 Ask everyone to come dressed as her favorite actress, and as each guest arrives, take a picture of her walking up your red carpet all glammed up. Then you'll have fun reminders of your evening!

6 Popcorn is a must!

Those are all great ideas, Friends, but what about NOT having your sleepover inside your house? Mom and Dad sometimes let me and my brother camp out in our RV parked in back of our house — it's got a mini TV and fridge and it's great fun. Or you could borrow a big tent and sleep in the backyard — a real laugh.

❝I once had a sleepover at a museum with five of my friends and my mom — we slept right under a dinosaur skeleton! — and it wasn't expensive at all.**❞**

Nice one, Princess. That sounds incredible. If you feel like being adventurous with your sleepover location, try phoning the bigger museums or other community groups for inspiration.

And now onward, Friends, to our final and most important W word!

Who to invite

So, you've got an idea of your budget, what the theme is going to be, and how many guests you can handle. The big decision that now faces you is, which of your trazillion friends are you gonna invite and who are you going to leave out? Princess, you know a thing or two about "etiquette" (fancy word for "rules"). Any thoughts?

Princess's pointers on the perilous pitfalls of the party guest list

1. Only invite people you know are going to get along – bickering is so not fun.

2. Invite people you want to invite, not people you feel you have to invite (because so-and-so invited you to theirs). Remember, it's YOUR party.

3. Remember that if you invite too many people, they may split off into smaller groups, which could cause

tension. Also, large numbers mean you have to look after your guests and may not be able to spend as much time relaxing and enjoying yourself – not good.

4. Instead of handing out your invitations in school and maybe upsetting those not invited, either mail them or send an e-mail invitation.

5. If you find out that a friend who wasn't invited is feeling left out, be honest and explain that you're only allowed limited numbers; then ask her to do something else with you, like going to a movie or shopping.

6. Send out your invitations well before your party so people have time to reply and also so they don't plan something else for that date.

Designing your invitations

The thing with any invitation is that it must give important information about where and when, etc.

66Duh! How obvious???**99**

Ahem, I am thinking here about a certain person's birthday party when that person forgot to put THE DATE of her party on the invitation. Ring any bells, Nora?

66 Ok, you got me...and don't call me that! Anyway, since then I've made some notes, which I'm happy to share with our Friend. **99**

Missy's no-mistakes invite info checklist
☺ Your name
☺ Your address
☺ Your phone number — so panicky parents have contact number
☺ Date, start time, and finish time — so panicky parents know when to pick up beloved daughter
☺ RSVP deadline — so you know how many guests are coming, and if someone can't come you've got time to invite someone else
☺ List of items you want each guest to bring, e.g.: sleeping bag + pillow + fanciest pjs/nightie + other fancy-dress costume in keeping with your theme if you're having one + toothbrush + flashlight + videos + DVD + CD + makeup + nail polish + body glitter + wigs(!) + any other stuff for makeovers

Awesome, Missy. That's the invitation contents figured out, but what about how the invitation looks? Ladies and, uhm, ladies, I now present:

How to make the best sleepover invites in the world . . . ever!

The mini-pillow invitation
What you need:
★ Plain white cardboard (4 inches by 3 inches; 10 cm x 8 cm for each invitation)
★ Cotton material — like a cut-up old pillowcase (10 inches by 7 inches; 25 cm x 18 cm for each invitation)
★ Cotton balls ★ Glue

What you do:
1 Place the cotton material pattern-side down (if it has a pattern!), and fold over a 3/4-inch (2 cm) hem down one of the longer edges. Then glue it down.
2 Turn your material over (so pattern is face up) and put a thin strip of glue along the edges of the other three sides.
3 Fold the material in half so that the two shorter ends meet, and press the gluey edges together.
4 Wait for the glue to dry, then turn your "pillowcase" inside out. If the material is patterned, this will now be on the outside.
5 Write your invitation on the card, (using glitter pens and gold stars to jazz it up). Stuff this into the pillowcase (trimming the card edges if necessary) and plump up your pillow with the cotton balls.

❝This sounds sooo cute!**❞**

❝Nah! Us sophisticated types think this next one is the cat's pajamas.**❞**

The jet-set invitation

The idea is that your invitation will look like one of those neat travel packs you get on really long airplane trips.

What you need:

★ Travel-size toothpaste tubes and brushes
★ Plastic sandwich bags — the ones with the zip-lock tops
★ Plain cardboard (about 5 inches by 3 inches for each invitation)

What you do:

1 Cut your card into a luggage-tag shape by cutting off two of the corners at one end, and drawing a "hole" at that end.

2 Write out your invitation on the tag.

Bubble, you're always going traveling with your folks. Maybe you can show our Friend what you'd put if you were doing a jet-set invitation?

❝No problem! OK, here's my invitation.**❞**

To: **Ms. Molly White**
(First-class passenger — make way!!!)
From: Bubble of 3 Cherry Tree Crescent, Dullsville
(In the Land of Bubbleonia)
Via: **Sleepover at my place**
(Please bring your own sleeping bag & pillow)
Arrive: **6 pm, Saturday, July 17**
Depart: 11 am, Sunday, July 18
Phone no.: 1-234-567-8900
Please confirm your seat (or bed!) by: July 5

Excellent stuff, Bubs! Now this is what you need to finish.

3 Put your toothpaste and toothbrush into the bag, along with the invitation, and "zip" shut.

4 (optional) If you're putting your jet-set invitation into an outer envelope, then decorate it with travel-themed graffiti.

Of course, you can have fun creating your own wacky invitation. . . .

The all-purpose invite

What you need:

Cardboard ★ Envelopes ★ Paint ★ Glue ★ Glitter ★ Plastic gemstones ★ Photos of your guests ★ Anything else you can think of!

What you do:

1 If you're having a theme for your sleepover, try to create a design based on that. For example, a star-shaped invitation is good for a Hollywood theme.

2 Personalize each guest's invitation by cutting out her face from a photo (if you haven't got a photo, sneakily ask her mom for one) and fixing it onto a picture of a celeb's body cut from a magazine. If you're feeling more artistic, you could draw the bodies with angel wings and a halo or devil horns and a tail — or whatever else inspires you!

3 Make your invitation a many-colored thing of glistening beauty by gluing on lots of glitter, plastic gemstones, and anything else pretty and sparkly you've got.

So, dear Friend, once you've figured out (or at least vaguely thought about!) when to have your party, where it's going to be, what the vibe's going to be, and who's coming, you can start to think about what we in the party-planning business call the, ahem, "cuisine."

66Yippeee! We're talking food — my very favorite subject!**99**

Scrumptious Sleepover Eats

66Ooh, I've got a recipe for pizza that our Friend must make!99

66Nothing compares to Missy's float-my-boat Coke.99

66I tell you, the way to impress your guests is with dips and crudités.99

66Crudy whats?!99

35

"Vegetable sticks."

"What's wrong with getting a pizza delivery?"

"I'm just thinking healthy, that's all!"

OK, Friends, cool it! Before we start arguing about what scrumptious suggestions to offer our Friend, we've got one problem left to deal with — the kitchen.

"What's wrong with the kitchen?"

In a word: Mom!

Moms and kitchens

The thing with moms (and the occasional dad) is that they get really nervous at the thought of you and your pals entering their kitchen. Their top three worries are that you will:

a) cut off your fingers

b) burn down the house

c) and — oh, the pain — make a "mess."

So, what's a girl to do?

"Ooh, I've got the answer to this one! I had a sleepover a couple of years ago and felt sure that me and the Friends were old enough to make our own food. This is the conversation I had with my mom a few days before my sleepover....**"**

Princess's step-by-step guide to getting your mom out of the kitchen and you in!

The scenario:

Princess: "Mom, I thought for my sleepover, we'd do dips to begin, baked potatoes with various fillings, and then a huge gooey sundae for dessert."

Mrs. Moxbury: "Lovely, sweetie. I'll be happy to do it."

66Here's how I solved the problem:**99**

1 Make your mom feel needed

Princess: "Well, it'd be great if you could help out with the shopping, but I thought me and the Friends would cook, since that's half the fun. Although I'd really, really appreciate it if you could be around, just in case — like, maybe relaxing in the living room."

2 The bribe

Princess: "Oh, look, speaking of which, I bought you that new magazine you wanted. You could read that, have a cup of coffee, and put your feet up for a change."

Mrs. M.: "But, but, but..."

3 The killer move

Princess: "Oh, and I've made a list of kitchen safety rules for your approval, which all the Friends have read and signed."

4 Put your mom into a state of shock

Mrs. M.: (shocked and stunned, taking list): "Uhm, I suppose so, hon. Thank you."

Princess's code of kitchen safety and accompanying parent-pleasing promises

Dear parents of _____ (your name here),
We, the undersigned, hereby promise to:

1. Be very careful when using sharp knives – cutting everything slowly and paying close attention.
2. Be very careful when handling hot stuff – always using oven mitts and moving slowly and carefully.
3. Call you if we have any problems.
4. Turn off appliances when not in use.
5. Not goof around too much.
6. Clean up as we go along.
7. Wash our hands.
8. Be very grateful that our dear friend _____ (your name here) has such an excellent and very groovy parent.

Signed _____

(you all sign here)

❝OK, now that you've got your mom taken care of, let's talk eats!**❞**

Calm down, Bubs, we're going to do that right now!

Now that you've talked your way into the kitchen, you'll be needing the Best Friends' recipes and tips for the all-time best sleepover cuisine for you to think about serving your guests. Drool on, Friend!

Hearty and wholesome: first courses

❝Ugh! Sounds like stuff my grandma would make me eat!**❞**

Don't worry, Bubs, these are the yummy dishes that will prepare our Friend's tummy for the gooey, luscious desserts that follow later! Actually, the first thing on the menu is pizza, and since you're the pizza queen, Bubs, I nominate you to be the first one to share your know-how with our Friend.

Bubble's awesome guide to pizza-eating

❝Pick up phone. Dial pizza place. Order. Wait. Pay delivery person. Eat pizza. Ha ha! Only joking! Ordering in pizza is cool, but it's expensive and nowhere near as much fun as making your own. So come on, Friend, let's bake!**❞**

Get your dough

❝There are two options here. Buy ready-made pizza crust from the supermarket or, for a really impressive (and yummier and super cheap) option, make your own dough before your guests arrive. Don't worry, it's easy as pie (no pun intended!).**❞**

The Best Friends' EZ pizza dough
For one biggy pizza or four small ones you will need:
★ 1/4 oz (7g) dry yeast ★ 7 1/2 oz (225 ml) warm water ★ One teaspoon sugar ★ One teaspoon salt ★ Two tablespoons olive oil ★ 1 1/2 cups (330 g) flour

What you do:

1 Preheat the oven to 425° F (220° C).

2 Dissolve the yeast in the water.

3 In a separate bowl, mix all the other ingredients, then put in the yeast mixture to bind it together.

4 On a floury surface, knead the dough by pushing and pulling it with clenched fists for five minutes. (It helps to think of an especially grouchy teacher at this point.)

5 Form the dough into a large ball. Rub a small amount of olive oil around a clean bowl, then put the dough into this bowl, covering it with a clean dish towel. Let the bowl sit somewhere warm for about 45 minutes. The yeast will make the dough rise and become spongy.

6 Grease a cookie sheet and then, with floured hands, roll dough out into a pizza shape, about a quarter of an inch (1 cm) thick.

7 When your friends arrive, stack on desired toppings (see pages 45–46).

8 Bake for 20–25 minutes. Totally scrumptious!

❝Hey, Bubble, can I tell our Friend about the most delicious veggie topping in the world, ever? You know, the 'Herbal Fluff' I invented at our last pizza feast?!**❞**

"Ooh, yeah. That's a good one!**"**

★ * ★ * * ★ * ★ * ★ * ★ * ★ * ★ * ★ * ★ * ★ * ★

Flower's herbal fluff pizza

"I love this because it's all light and creamy and the herbs give it a really subtle flavor.**"**

What you need:

★ Small container ricotta cheese (or other soft cream cheese) ★ One tablespoon olive oil ★ A few torn-up basil leaves or sprinkle of dried basil (about half a teaspoon) ★ Sprinkle of oregano (like, just a quarter of a teaspoon) ★ One clove garlic, chopped (optional) ★ One tomato, sliced ★ Big handful of grated cheese (mozzarella or cheddar)

What you do:

1 Mix together chopped garlic, ricotta, oil, and basil, and spread over pizza crust.

2 Put on tomato, sprinkle on oregano, and cover with grated cheese.

Slap it on, mama-mia!

❝This one makes everyone happy! Each person gets her own individual pizza crust and then throws on whatever she wants from the following ingredients (deep breath):**❞**

Meats: sausage, pepperoni, crisp bacon, cooked and chopped chicken, cooked meatballs.

Fish: tuna, shrimp, scallops, fish sticks, anchovies.

❝Anchovies! Ugh! How totally gross!**❞**

Veggies: tomato, peppers, mushroom, sweet corn, onion, scallions, artichoke (very classy!), cooked spinach.

Cheese: mozzarella (can't be beat for stringiness), cheddar, parmesan (smells icky, but tastes yummy), edam, blue cheese...in fact, ALL cheeses are acceptable. Hurray!

Other stuff: tomato purée (or any other thick tomato sauce), pesto sauce, sprinkles of dried oregano or basil, black pepper, olives, garlic, chilies (but go easy there!), BBQ sauce (very tasty with chicken!), capers, pineapple, egg (either boiled and chopped or dropped raw in the center before it goes in the oven — make sure it's cooked all the way through before you eat it, though!).

"Get each of your guests to do a 'pizza portrait' of someone else. The results are crazy! Here's one I did of Princess.**"**

Molly's pizza Princess portrait

1 For her light complexion, I used ricotta cheese covered in grated mozzarella.

2 For her big eyes, I got two mushrooms, removed the stalks, and put them cap-side down.

3 Her lovely lips were made with slices of red pepper.

4 Two juicy slices of tomato became her gorgeous cheeks.

5 Her nose was made from a little chunk of sausage.

6 Finally, her beautiful strawberry-blond hair was created with strips of cheddar smeared lightly with tomato puree.

66Hmm, thanks for that — I think. Anyway, now that we've done pizza, I want to tell you about those crudités and dips.99

66Boo! 'Healthy' food. Bore-ring!99

"Ooh, you sassy girl! I remember you scoffing down your share at my last sleepover. In case anyone else thinks like Bubble, I guarantee they are wonderfully munchy AND they don't make you feel sick! I've dedicated these two recipes to their greatest fans.**"**

Hippie-dippy hummus for Flower
For four people, you need:

★ One can chickpeas ★ One garlic clove, finely chopped ★ Two tablespoons tahini paste (made from sesame seeds and available in most supermarkets, but you could replace it with a couple of spoons of peanut butter) ★ One lemon ★ Two tablespoons olive oil ★ Two tablespoons water

What you do:

1 Drain chickpeas and (**after** *telling Mom or Dad what you're up to*) whirl them in a blender with juice from the lemon, chopped garlic, and tahini paste (or peanut butter). If you haven't got a blender, place ingredients in a large bowl and mash them up with a potato masher or fork (take turns when your arm aches!).

2 Drizzle in the olive oil and water until your hummus reaches a "dippy" consistency.

★ * ★ * ★ * ★ * ★ * ★ * ★ ★ * ★ * ★ ★ * ★ * ★ *

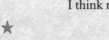

Gorgeous guacamole for Golly Ms. Molly

> **"**Is there a finer dip known to girlkind? I think not!**"**

★

For four people, you need:
★ One large ripe avocado (has to be ripe!) ★ Two scallions, chopped ★ One garlic clove, finely chopped ★ One tomato (or a couple of scoops from a can of chopped tomatoes) ★ One lime or half a lemon ★ Dash of chili sauce (optional)

★   ★

What you do:
1 Drop tomato into cup of boiling water (careful, now!).
2 Peel and roughly chop avocado and place in a bowl, pour over squeezed juice from lime or lemon (this keeps

avocado from turning yucky gray color), and add scallions and garlic. Mush together, using a potato masher or a fork.

3 Take tomato from cup and remove skin — give it a gentle squeeze and it should peel off easily. Chop skinned tomato into smallish chunks, and stir into guacamole with a dash of the chili sauce.

What a delicious couple of dips, Princess. One question, though – what should we dip? Time for a vote!

The Best Friends' top five dunkers

For dipping, we hereby declare the winners as follows:

1 Veggie sticks (sliced peppers, carrots, celery, cucumber)

2 Toasted pita bread cut into wedges

3 Tortilla chips

4 Bread sticks

5 Your fingers (gross, but true!)

WATCH IT, Friend! Keep those hands clean — especially when cooking or putting fingers into dips!

And finally, here comes the...

Best dag-nabbit sandwich known to girlkind!!!

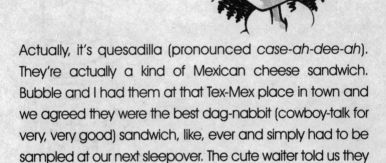

❝Best what?❞

Actually, it's quesadilla (pronounced *case-ah-dee-ah*). They're actually a kind of Mexican cheese sandwich. Bubble and I had them at that Tex-Mex place in town and we agreed they were the best dag-nabbit (cowboy-talk for very, very good) sandwich, like, ever and simply had to be sampled at our next sleepover. The cute waiter told us they were totally easy to make and gave us this recipe:

Cute waiter's quesadilla recipe
To make one sandwich (serves two), you need:
★ Two flour tortillas ★ Two handfuls grated cheese
★ Pat of butter

What you do:

1 Heat butter in large frying pan and swish around.

2 Put one tortilla on a plate and spread cheese over it to the edges.

3 Place second tortilla on top.

4 Carefully transfer your sandwich to the pan (be careful it doesn't fall apart; slide a spatula underneath and use your spare hand to keep the top on).

5 Cook for a couple of minutes on each side (you want the cheese to be melted and the tortillas lightly browned). Cut into four delicious pieces.

And if that's not the best sandwich in the West, I'll eat my ten-gallon hat!

"You can also add loads of other things to the cheese — like onions, sausage, tomatoes, and sandwich pickle. Yee-haw!**"**

* * * * * * * * * * * * * * * * * * *

Something to slurp: beverages and such

From ice-cream floats to dessert-in-a-glass cocktails...what would a sleepover be without someone somewhere making a rad concoction in a glass? These are the BFs' faves. (Big straws are a must for top slurrrpability!)

Princess's island delight

What you need:

★ 2 oz (60 ml) coconut milk ★ Small can pineapple chunks ★ Four ice cubes' worth of crushed ice (put in plastic bag and crush with rolling pin) ★ Whipped cream and cherry (optional)

What you do:

Mix everything together in a blender. Or, if you haven't got a blender, use a can of crushed pineapple or 5 oz can (150 ml) of pineapple juice (although it won't be quite as slushy!). Top with whipped cream and a cherry, if you've got them.

"Looks and tastes luscious!**"**

"Do you remember when we made these and your mom gave us those teeny-tiny umbrellas to stick in our glasses?**"**

★ * ★ * ★ * ★ * ★ * ★ * ★ * ★ * ★ * ★ * ★ * ★ *

Flower's healing smoothie

What you need:

★ One frozen banana (or fresh if you don't have a blender) ★ Two handfuls of soft fresh fruit (strawberries, melon, kiwi, etc.) ★ 6 oz (170 ml) fruit juice (any kind)

What you do:

Mix it all up in the blender, pour, sip, and think peaceful thoughts! (If you don't have a blender, mash the fruit with a potato masher, adding the juice slowly as you go.)

66After our field trip last year, I felt exhausted, but after Flower made me one of these smoothies I felt like I could run a marathon!99

Missy's float-my-boat Coke

What you need: cola ★ vanilla ice cream

What you do: Half-fill tall glass with cola. Top with two scoops of ice cream.

66A friend of mine does this with cream soda and strawberry ice cream — it's so dreamy. Sweet, but dreamy.99

66What's next? Personally, I think our Friend will need tons of sweet stuff at her sleepover. Whaddya think, Molly?!99

You've got it, Bubble.

Sweet gooey glory: sundaes!

Me and my Best Friends agree that when it comes to sleepover sundaes you just have to have the ultimate experience, otherwise known as (cue thriller-movie-style sound effect) dun dun dun...

The Abominable Sundae!!

The Abominable is a mix of four key sundae ingredients. You need at least one from each of the following categories, but you can use as many as you like.

1 Frozen stuff: ice cream, frozen yogurt, or sorbet.

2 Gooey syrups: chocolate, fudge, raspberry, or strawberry sauce, maple syrup, and (Best Friends' fave) melted chocolate bars (see box).

3 Mix-ins: broken-up cookies, crushed chocolate bars, squishy fruit, cereals, and sweets.

4 Fancy finishes: hot-chocolate powder (sprinkled), maraschino cherries, shaved chocolate, sprinkles (like hundreds and thousands, chopped nuts, etc.).

The messy business of melting chocolate bars

66 OK, so melting perfectly good chocolate bars is the kinda thing only the most twisted of adolescent chocoholics will try. But I promise you, Friend, once you've mastered the art, there's not a dish in the land that can't be improved with a yummy bunch of chocolate gloop! **99**

To melt chocolate:

Use a double-boiler or the old saucepan-and-bowl trick, like here —

1 Heat a saucepan half filled with water until the water bubbles a bit.

2 Place on top of the saucepan a ceramic or glass bowl that's a bit larger than the saucepan. The bowl should touch the water but *not* the bottom of the pan.

3 Break up chocolate into pieces and put into bowl.

4 Turn heat down low and stir chocolate occasionally as it melts.

Note: If your bar is solid chocolate, it will take around three to four minutes to melt. But if your chosen bar has things mixed in with the chocolate — toffee, caramel, nuts, etc. — it will take around five to eight minutes to melt. Overheating causes chocolate to go stiff and weird — if this happens, add a little cream or vegetable oil and continue melting the chocolate until it's smooth.

* Be *very careful* when handling pans of boiling water.
* To avoid spilling the boiling water, put the pan in the sink before trying to remove the bowl containing the chocolate.
* Always use oven mitts when handling hot things.
* Melted chocolate can be very hot — wait till it cools before eating so you won't burn your mouth or fingers.

To do The Abominable:

1 Get the biggest bowl you can find in the house and lay out whatever you've got of the four key ingredients. All gather around the bowl.

2 Put in scoops of as many kinds of frozen stuff as you've got.

3 Smother with whatever gooey syrup you want.

4 Everyone add her favorite mix-ins at once — then squish them into the ice cream with the back of your spoons.

5 Garnish with as much whipped cream and fancy finishes as possible.

6 Grab spoon, crowd around bowl, and dig in!

❝ Ugh, all that talk of gooey chocolate has made me feel sick. **❞**

Oh, no, not again! Poor Flower, she always gets queasy even after the tiniest bit of scrumptious sleepover eats. So, let's put on our thinking cap for a moment, and figure out what we should do if one of you starts feeling a little sick.

Molly has a quiet word about feeling queasy

* Get some air — either take a stroll outside or sit by an open window.
* Sip some water.
* Focus on something else — try watching a video or chat quietly.
* Don't panic if you do throw up — if it's because you ate too much, you'll usually begin to feel better within an hour. But you should definitely call for a parent's help if this happens.

❝ Thanks, Molly. Actually, I am feeling a little better now. Let's go on! **❞**

❝And now for my fave kinda food — quick-fix stuff for girls who wanna get on with the party! Friends, we give you...**❞**

No-fuss movie munchies and all-night snack attacks ★ ★

Tex-Mex popcorn

What you need:

★ Big bowl of freshly popped popcorn (equal to about 5 oz (150 g) of pre-popped corn) ★ One tablespoon of taco seasoning ★ 2 oz (60 g) butter ★ 3 oz (85 g) grated cheddar cheese

❝Do you remember that time we put chopped jalapeño peppers in, not realizing how hot they were? We had to drink cold milk for about three hours afterward!**❞**

❝And then my brother thought it was leftovers and finished three huge bites before the chili hit!**❞**

What you do:

1 Put popcorn in large bowl.

2 Melt the butter in the microwave for 15–30 seconds on high, or heat it in a small pan on the stove.

3 Stir in the seasoning and mix in with the popcorn and cheese.

Caramel popcorn

"Serve as a follow-up to the Tex-Mex: a winning double snack!**"**

What you need:

★ Big bowl of freshly popped popcorn (equal to about 5 oz (150 g) of pre-popped corn) ★ 4 oz (110 g) butter (leave it out of the fridge, so it's not rock hard) ★ 4 oz (110 g) dark brown sugar

What you do:

1 Mash butter with wooden spoon, then add the brown sugar and beat until the sugar is combined and the mixture is light and creamy.

2 Toss popcorn with butter mixture in a large roasting pan, then put it in preheated oven (around 375° F (190° C) for about eight minutes or until crispy.

66 I love this next one because it's so much classier than your typical junky snack! **99**

66 Said like a true princess! And she's right — even I feel totally sophisticated eating these. **99**

Chocolate-dipped strawberries
What you need:
★ Small basket of strawberries (leave the stems on) ★ Two medium-sized chocolate bars (white, plain, or milk!) ★ 2 oz (60 g) butter

What you do:
1 Wash and dry strawberries.
2 Melt chocolate (see page 57) with the butter, giving it a good stir.

3 Hold strawberry by stem and dip it into the chocolate. Lift out with a twist and place it on a plate lined with waxed paper. Repeat with the rest of the strawberries.

4 Put them in the fridge until chocolate sets (usually about an hour).

If you can't wait for the chocolate to set, use the warm chocolate as a dip, with everyone doing their own dunking (you gotta be quick before it sets – but be sure it's not too hot before putting it into your mouth).

Of course, dear Friend, you'll probably want to offer some chips and nuts at your party. But there are so many different kinds, and different brands, how is a girl supposed to decide which ones to spend her cash on?! Avoid a snack crisis with our simple but genius snack-o-meter.

Before your sleepover, ask each of your guests what her favorite snacks are in order of preference. Award each snack the following points:

No. 1 favorite snack = 5 points ★ No. 2 snack = 4 points ★ No. 3 snack = 3 points ★ No. 4 snack = 2 points ★ No. 5 snack = 1 point

Count up each snack's score and figure out the top five. Then fill in the snack-o-meter below. You will then know which snacks to buy for your guests! Clever, huh? (Or just do it on the night of your sleepover — having bought a good selection beforehand.)

The Best Friends' packet snack-o-meter

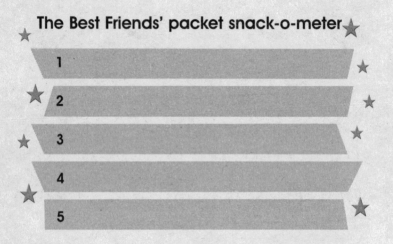

1

2

3

4

5

OK, BFs. What are your favorites?

66 Bite-sized pretzels — the saltier, the better. They're funky! **99**

“Garlicky tortilla chips — because they remind me of when I went to Spain.**”**

“Smoky BBQ kettle chips — they're simply marvelous, darling.**”**

“Pistachio nuts — it's fun to crack them open, they're delicious, and they're good for you!**”**

I can't believe none of you mentioned cheese puffs, surely the most glorious of all the world's snacks? No? Just me? Oh, well, moving on. . . .

Sending your guests off with a breakfast banquet fit for a queen

Ha! Not really! Truth is, you'll probably be too tired from the night before to cook an actual banquet! Any thoughts, Friends?

66 The easiest thing to do is to put out a few well-chosen items and let your hungry friends grab what they want. Like this... 99

Princess's (and Bubble's) essential top-ten breakfast items

1 Orange juice

2 Doughnuts

3 Pop-up waffles...

4 ...with maple syrup

5 Toasted bagels...

6 ...with cream cheese

7 Chocolate croissants

8 Vanilla yogurt

9 Bananas

10 Leftover pizza (Bubble insisted I include it)

❝Nothing tastier than last night's pizza for breakfast!**❞**

Mmm! Thank you, Princess and, uhm, Bubble.

So, Friend, that's our top food tips for you. You're probably thinking that a sleepover with such superior eats can get no better — but that's because you haven't yet read about our amazing plans for entertaining your bedazzled guests. Read on, and find out how to get your sleepover really jumping.

Stuff to Do

"All the best sleepovers have a scary storytelling session."

"I hate that part! My favorite thing is makeovers — I still laugh when I think about when we turned Molly into Frankenstein last Halloween!"

"Don't listen to them, Friend — the best things are music, dancing, and silly games!"

OK, BFs, TURN THE VOLUME DOWN! I need to have a quiet word with our new Friend.

Molly has a quiet word about doing stuff

Now, dear Friend, what the BFs are trying to say (in their confused and loud way) is that there are loads of different activities you can do to keep your guests entertained. You probably won't manage to do them all, but you need to decide before your party begins what stuff you'd like to do and then make the necessary pre-party preparations. Otherwise, you might decide you want to do something and find out you can't because you don't have the right equipment (e.g., for karaoke) — and then arguments break out among your guests about what they want to do, and your sleepover soon becomes a "sulkover." Yikes!

The five best games for sleepovers (in reverse order)

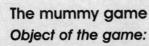

The mummy game
Object of the game:

To be the fastest team to turn a player into a mummy (not the kind that sits in an armchair and worries, but the spooky kind from Egypt).

What you need:

★ Four rolls of toilet paper

What you do:
1 Split into two teams. Each team is armed with two new rolls of toilet paper.

2 Nominate a mummy.

3 The first team to completely wrap their mummy wins!

Pre-party prep: Make sure you've got stacks of toilet rolls!

"Everyone always wants me to be the mummy because I'm short, so I don't take up much paper! Still, at least I'm usually on the winning team!**"**

Best Friends
TOP TIP

Play some lively music during the game — it will add to the fun! Also, be sure to take a picture of each team posing with their finished mummy.

The kissy-kissy poster game
Object of the game:

To be the girl who plants a kiss nearest to the celeb's luscious lips.

What you need:

★ Poster of boy-celeb ★ Sticky Tac ★ Horrible-colored lipstick

What you do:

1 Put a poster of your fave male celebrity on the wall.

2 Before each girl's turn, paint her lips really thickly with the brightest lipstick you've got.

3 Blindfold her and spin her around five times.

4 Point her in the direction of the poster and get her to smooch away!

5 The girl whose lips are closest to the celeb's mouth gets to keep the lipstick-covered poster as her prize.

Pre-party prep: Go through your old magazines to get posters and ask Mom for old lipstick.

Boogie Woogie dance competition!
Object of the game:
Each team competes for the Boogie Cup by making up a cool dance routine.

What you need:
★ Stereo or boom box ★ A couple of dance music CDs ★ Wacky costumes (optional) ★ Any other crazy props you might want to use in your dance ★ The Boogie Cup (it's great to have a real prize to give out, but it shouldn't be expensive — an el-cheapo mug or fake-crystal glass would be really funny)

What you do:
1 Divide into teams (pairs are good).
2 Give each team twenty minutes to come up with their dance routine.
3 If everyone is going to dance to the same song, keep replaying it while everyone is rehearsing. If each team wants different songs, take turns rehearsing while the others get to do something else.
4 The hostess (you!) decides who the winners are.

Best Friends TOP TIP

Video each team's efforts (if your family doesn't have a camcorder, try to borrow one for the evening – it'll be worth it!) and watch the video in the morning as your breakfast entertainment.

❝Missy is a brilliant dancer and nearly always wins. Why not share a few tips with our Friend, Missy?❞

❝You got it!❞

Missy's dance class
Keep it low'n'funky!

If you want to get that urban, hip-hop look, keep your hips way low and your knees bent slightly. It's all in the 'tude, girl!

Perfect the body ripple!

You know the move — the one they do in the pop videos where it looks as though an invisible force is passing through the dancer's body? It looks so professional and yet it's sooo simple to do.

1 Stand with your feet and knees together — with your body relaxed, almost slumped.

2 Flex your knees slightly, bend forward at the waist, and tuck your head down so your chin is touching your chest.

3 Push your knees forward, followed by your hips. (As you do this, your upper body will start to become upright again — still keep your chin tucked in.)

4 Allow your top half to tilt backward slightly but stay balanced as you keep pushing your hips forward.

5 Finish by releasing your chin as your head flicks backward. You are now perfectly upright.

6 Keep practicing, take it slowly, and think of yourself as a big gloppy milkshake — you'll soon master it!

Coordinate, Friend

If there are two of you, think of how you're standing in relation to one another — try back-to-back or face-to-face and keep your moves the same — it'll look really neat (try coordinating a ripple!). Don't try anything too complicated. Just try repeating a series of moves, maybe using more of your space each time.

Camp it up! (Molly *always* does this one!)

Sing the lyrics of the song with some dramatic "interpretations." For example, if it's a mushy love song, stick your hand under your top and push the material forward in time to the music so it looks as if your heart is beating. Try using some silly props — grab those balloons and experiment!

Wild rock-out (Bubble *always* does this one!)

Can't dance? Won't dance? Simple. Jump up and down as wildly as you can, shaking your head back and forth and roaring like a hungry dinosaur. Spectators will be stunned by the, ahem, *energy* of your performance.

 Jumping up and down after having huge quantities of sleepover eats is a sure way to make you sick to your stomach. Our advice? Let your food go down before you *get* down.

 ## Karaoke Queen
Object of the game:

To be the sweetly singing girl who wins the Karaoke Queen Crown.

What you need:

★ Basic karaoke machine or karaoke CD and printed lyrics ★ Fancy dress (optional) ★ Plastic tiara for the winning queen (optional!)

What you do:

1 Each girl belts out a song of her choice, following the printed lyrics — and trying not to lose her place — as the instrumental recording plays.

2 Each Friend votes for her favorite act (*not* herself). If there's a tie, the hostess breaks it with her vote!

3 Don't forget to video everything — including the crowning "ceremony"!

Pre-party prep: Get a karaoke machine. Borrow one if you can, or rent one locally. Or else, karaoke CDs, tapes, DVDs, and videos come complete with printed lyrics and don't cost too much. Buy cheap prize (optional).

Hang on, the Friends' reigning Karaoke Queen would like to say something. . . .

Princess's perfect sleepover theme

I love karaoke. (Did I mention I'm pretty good?) Anyway, for my last birthday sleepover, I had a disco and karaoke theme. Let me tell you what I did...

1 I made the dining room into my dance hall and sleeping room by clearing out the table and chairs.

2 I strung up lots of silver tinsel and gold and silver balloons.

3 I made my own glitter ball by hanging a large beach ball covered in tin foil from the center of the ceiling. Then I got two gooseneck lamps — one with a red bulb and one with a blue bulb — and put them in opposite corners of the room, pointing them up at the ball.

4 For the karaoke contest, Mom and Dad borrowed some plastic orange crates and lined them up against one wall to make a "stage."

5 Then, for a laugh, I got a huge piece of thick, white cardboard, painted an almost life-size picture of a rad rock chick's body, cut out a hole for the head and put it up on stage. Everyone had a turn at sticking her face through the hole and having her picture taken! The results were hilarious!

And what a fabulous evening that was, Princess!

OK! And now the moment we've all been waiting for. Friend, here is . . .

The number one sleepover game of all time: Truth or Dare!!!

Object of the game:

To get your friends to confess to funny or silly secrets.

What you do:

1 Sit in a circle and take turns picking a Truth or a Dare.

2 A Truth means you have to answer a question honestly.

3 A Dare means doing a nutty trick.

Important Rules:

Don't be mean! This is supposed to be a fun game, so don't try to upset someone or make her do a trick that could harm her.

Everyone should agree that all the secrets will be treated as top secret and will NOT be repeated as gossip at school.

Pre-party prep: It will help the game run smoothly if you write out "Truths" and "Dares" on slips of paper and put them in two hats (or whatever!) first. It will also make the game much more fair.

The BFs' sample Truths and Dares to get you started

★ *TRUTHS*

★ When was the last time you picked your nose?

★ What is the meanest thing you've ever said about someone?

★ Who is your most embarrassing relative and why?

★ Describe the last fight you had.

★ If you had to get married tomorrow, who would you marry (NO celebrities!)?

★ If you could change one thing about the way you look, what would it be and why?

★ What is the most disgusting thing you've ever done?

★ Pick a word beginning with W to describe yourself.

★ What is the lamest present you've ever been given?

★ Have you ever kissed — or even thought about kissing — a boy? Who? If not, who would you kiss if you HAD to?

★ When was the last time you lied? Who to and why?

★ Which celebrity is the person sitting on your left most like?

★ Tell us a secret.

★ Tell us about something you regret doing.

★ DARES

★ Sniff the person on your right's toes. Describe the smell.

★ Sing a song all the way through.

★ Find a teddy bear and have a pretend argument with him/her for one minute.

★ In a French accent, tell the person on your left that you love her and want to marry her.

★ Do a song and dance impression of a current pop singer.

★ Find the brightest lipstick you can and — shutting your eyes — give yourself rosy cheeks and pouty lips.

★ Open the window and shout (or whisper loudly if it's late): "____ (your name) is the most beautiful girl in all the world!"

★ Put a pair of underwear on your head and leave them there for three minutes. Giggling adds an extra minute.

★ Using a sock for a nose, pretend you are an elephant by crawling all around the room, swishing your "trunk" and trumpeting as you go.

★ Give yourself a big behind by putting your pillow under your nightie/PJ bottoms, then ask each person in the room separately, "Does my backside look big in this?"

★ Make the ugliest face you can, then pucker up and kiss the person of your choice.

★ Burrow into your sleeping bag, then pretend to be a beautiful butterfly emerging from your old caterpillar body, and finish by "flying" around the room and singing "Tra-la-la-la — just look at my lovely wings!" over and over.

And now, Friend, after all those contests, I think it's time for you and your guests to relax and treat yourselves to . . .

Makeovers and other pampering pastimes

One of the many great things about being a girl is that you get to spend hours making yourself even more gorgeous than you already are, at the same time as you're having fun with your girlfriends! OK, let's beautify! Friends, what've you got?

" At Missy's last sleepover, she did a manicure on each of us. All our nails looked amazing and we felt really glam. I think she should share her trade secrets with our Friend. Missy, how about it? **"**

" No probs. Anything for our Friend! **"**

Missy's miracle five-minute manicure

What you need:

★ Soap ★ Moisturizer or hand lotion ★ Nail file/emery board ★ Nail clippers/scissors ★ Nail polish

What you do:

30 secs: Soak hands in warm soapy water and dry.

10 secs: Moisturize all over hands with the lotion.

1 min 50 secs: Trim nails, and file into a gently rounded shape or a trendier, squarer shape (ask your "client" what she'd prefer) using gentle strokes in one direction, toward the center of the nail.

2 mins 30 secs: The tricky painting part. Apply a small amount of polish to your brush. Paint one stroke down the center of your nail, then use one stroke down each of the two sides of your nail. Bingo! Fab nails in no time!

❝Fast or what, huh?! It's the same for your feet, but remember to wedge cotton balls between your toes to keep the polish from smudging — and it it feels grrrreeaat! Also try different colors (like three different stripes on one nail!) or buy some groovy nail transfers for your guests.**❞**

* ★ * ★ * ★ * ★ * ★ * ★ * ★ * ★ * ★ * ★ * ★ *

Flower's Fruity face masks

❝Try one of my homemade face masks. They get rid of all the dirt and grime from deep within your skin and leave you feeling really zingy!**❞**

Lime and yogurt

❝This one cleanses and moisturizes oily skin.**❞**

What you need:

★ One teaspoon lime juice ★ One teaspoon orange juice ★ Half a small carton plain yogurt (unsweetened)

Mix ingredients together, smear on face, and leave for five minutes. Then rinse off.

Banana and egg

❝This one nourishes the skin and tightens pores.**❞**

What you need:

★ One ripe banana ★ One egg yolk ★ Two teaspoons almond oil (optional)

Mix ingredients thoroughly with a fork. Smear on face, wait ten minutes, and rinse off.

❝While you're lying back waiting for your face pack to do its work, try putting a couple of cold, damp, used tea bags or slices of cucumber on your (closed!) eyes — it takes away any puffiness and makes your eyes sparkle!**❞**

Best Friends
TOP TIP

Create the effect of a beauty parlor by laying towels on a bed. Pick one or two of you to be pampered by the others; put on relaxing music and serve beverages from page 53 while your "clients" get their treatments.

❝This has all got far too fem! Where's the fun gone?!**❞**

Who says you can't be fem and have a laugh? Don't you remember what fun we had when we did you up as a celebrity, Bubble? Which reminds me...

How to do celebrity makeovers

Once you're feeling gorgeous and clean, and your nails are looking totally sophisticated, it's time for some serious makeover action! Here's what to do:

1 Ask your guests to bring some makeup, hair accessories, flamboyant clothes, and lots of recent magazines to the sleepover. Scrounge old makeup and stuff from your mom and her friends (women always have loads they never use). Dump everything you've got into a big pile on the floor.

2 Take a "before" photo of everyone. (If you don't have a camera, get one of those disposable ones with a built-in flash.)

3 Pick a partner — one of you is going to make over the other one and vice versa.

4 Hunt through the magazines for pictures of the celeb your partner most wants to look like. But don't tell the others what celeb you are doing.

5 Using your genius creative skills, change your partner into her chosen celeb!

6 After everyone is done, see if you can guess who everyone is supposed to be. If it's not obvious who they are, turn it into a game by asking ten questions to which the "celeb" can answer only yes or no.

7 Take your "after" photos — it'll make everyone feel very glam and it will be hysterical comparing them to the before pictures.

Some more creative girl things

If you're anything like me or Flower — for example, a mushy sensitive type who talks baby-talk to kittens, etc. — my guess is you're the kind of girl who likes to have a reminder of awesome events such as your fab sleepover.

Here are our two best ideas for utterly groovy, craftsy things for you to make and keep.

Flower's Fab Fun-Fur Flip-Flops

❝The fur lining makes them feel super luxurious. They're so easy to make, even your brother could do it!!!**❞**

What you need:

★ A cheap pair of flip-flops ★ Fun fur (animal print, Day-Glo — whatever you like) ★ Sequins ★ Glue

What you do:

1 Place the flip-flops on the back side of the fun fur. Draw around the bottoms of the flip-flops and then cut out the shape in the fur. Make sure you have one left foot and one right foot!

2 Take each fun-fur cutout and, laying it over the correct flip-flop, use a pen to mark the three places where the strap joins the insole.

3 Now make a cut from the outer rim of the fun fur to where your pen marks are.

4 Smear each flip-flop's insole with glue, then carefully fix on your fun fur — it's easier if you start at the heel and roll the fun fur out up to the toe, adjusting it around the straps. The slits you made should now be hidden by the close fit of the insole and the shagginess of the fur!
5 Glue sequins along the straps and leave to dry.

Molly's groovily graffitied pillowcases

What you need:
★ A white pillowcase for each of you ★ Bunch of fabric marker pens

What you do:
1 Each of you write the same slogan across the top of your pillowcase so you're united in your theme, something like: "I made it through a night with Missy during Spring Vacation!"

❝Gee! Thanks!❞

2 Personalize your pillowcase with a self-portrait and some in-jokes from your evening and get everyone to sign it. Then write goofy stuff on everyone else's.

Miscellaneous messing around

Enough of the nice stuff, Friend. Now it's time we told you about some midnight monkey business!

"Ha ha! I like the sound of this!"

"I'm not sure I do — this stuff makes me nervous. We're not talking about anything too scary, are we, Molly?"

Nah...well, not yet, tee-hee! First, though, let's tell our Friend about our favorite pranks — a very traditional sleepover pastime.

The Best Friends' top five sleepover pranks

1 Put strips of bubble wrap between the toilet seat and the toilet rim. The first guest who sits on the toilet will get a loud surprise.

2 After the first girl has fallen asleep, everybody agree to convince her the next morning that she was talking in her sleep about her deep love for the teacher she dislikes the most.

3 Choose someone who's a heavy sleeper. Then, once she's fast asleep, give her two big rosy dolly cheeks using an old lipstick. If she's a really heavy sleeper, you could go for a curly mustache. Just make sure that whatever you use (eyeliner or face paint) is easy to wash off!

4 Double wrap a big lump of cream cheese (or similar squishy stuff) in plastic sandwich bags and leave it where someone will walk on it when they get up in the morning. No harm will be done, but she won't think that at first!

5 Wait for the first person to fall asleep, then the rest of you wave a strong-smelling perfume or deodorant under her nose. In a whisper, ask your sleeping friend any question you want. When she wakes up, tell her what you asked her and what she answered.

"Can I please tell our Friend about our latest versions of the traditional sleepover pillow fight?**"**

If you must, Bubs!

Bubble's rowdy variations on the pillow fight

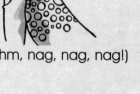

Silly-string fight
Arm yourself with a can of silly string and attack, attack, attack! (Probably best done outdoors, just in case Mom decides to, uhm, nag, nag, nag!)

Balloon stomp

You'll probably have loads of balloons around, so it would be a shame not to make good use of 'em! Just tie a couple of balloons to everybody's ankles with a piece of string, then run around trying to burst everyone's balloons (by stomping *only*) before they get yours. Stomptastic fun!

WATCH IT, Friend! Remember, it's only a game! There's no need to be too rough and rowdy. Make it a rule that bullying isn't allowed!

And finally, Friend, after the food's been eaten, games played, pranks done, and makeovers, uhm, made over, darkness falls, an owl hoots in the distance, and a floorboard creaks.... Be scared, be very scared, because it's ...

Scary story time!

❝I wanna go h-h-home!**❞**

Aw, come on, Flower, it's a must to tell a few chilling stories at your sleepover. And, anyway, the Best Friends are nice girls — we're not in the habit of stressing you or anyone else out. Sleepovers are supposed to be fun, so with that in mind, Princess has come up with the following rules:

Princess's code of conduct for (nicely) scaring each other

THE NUMBER ONE RULE: no scary films, seances, or ouija board games. Not because the ghosties will come and get you, but because – with a little imagination and the excitement of the evening – you could become very freaked out and turn into a babbling wreck.
Not a good look for a girl.

THE NUMBER TWO RULE: no mean tricks that could make a girl think she was being chased by a monster out to hurt her. For instance, locking her out (too dangerous), picking on her, waking her in her sleep, etc.

Remember, keep the scary stories light. You wanna still be able to laugh through your chattering teeth, right? Then try telling a few urban-myth type stories.

OK, Princess, let's give our Friend an idea of what kind of scary story is cool for sleepovers. Got one handy?

❝I sure have. This is one I heard recently on the Internet. It goes something like this:**❞**

The mysterious hitchhiker

Sally was thirteen and on a vacation with her father, Sam. It was the first time they'd been away since the tragic death of Sally's mom, Teresa, the summer before. Her dad had thought it would be good to rent a car and just drive wherever the road took them. One dusky evening, as they were driving through

---

the Arizona desert, with no sign of civilization for miles and miles, they saw a shadowy figure standing by the side of the road. As they got closer, they saw it was a tall, bearded man with piercing eyes, who was holding out his thumb hitching a ride. Although Sam was a cautious man, something made him stop and pick up the stranger. The man got into the car and just stared straight ahead. Sam made loads of small talk, but the man didn't say a word until he asked them to stop the car. They were still in the middle of nowhere! Sam pulled over. The stranger turned to Sam and Sally and said, "Teresa loves you both very much." Then he got out of the car. When Sally and Sam looked back — he was gone. Sam was totally spooked, so he reported the incident to the sheriff in the next town they came to. The sheriff sighed, and explained that it was the fifth time the mysterious hitchhiker had shown up that month and passed on a cryptic message before vanishing.

 Hang on ... was he a real person or a ghost?

Aha! We may never know!

So, Friend, have you got your sleepover superplan in place yet? Know what you're eating? Worked out your evening's entertainments? Whaddya mean, "No!"??? Oh, dear, Friend, it sounds like you need the doubt-busting BFs to blow away your remaining party problems! Let's move on to the next chapter and a worry-free sleepover!

Your Sleepover Problems Solved

Can't decide who to invite? Plagued by annoying brothers? Quarrelsome friends? We've been there.... And now we're here to help you! Fire away, readers!

Dad dread

Dear Best Friends,

My name is Ella. I have tried everything I can think of to get my parents to let me have a sleepover, and they just say, "No. Out of the question." My dad says he doesn't want to be wakened all night and Mom just sides with him. The thing is, I've been to all my friends' houses and now I'm getting really embarrassed that I haven't been allowed to invite anyone to mine. I'm dreading the next sleepover invitation I get, knowing I'll never be able to return the favor. What would you do?

Ella, 10, Philadelphia

What the Best Friends say

As your Best Friends, Ella, we assure you that we love and care for you and DO NOT judge you by your party-giving abilities! I'm sure your other friends wouldn't want you to worry about it either. If the parent people are against a sleepover, try one of the BFs get-together ideas from page 116 instead.

I'm always around Princess's or Missy's. I used to feel a little guilty, but now I see that there are always going to be some girls who are better equipped (with bigger houses, more sympathetic parents, etc.) to do the sleepover hostess thing. Enjoy being a guest — you get all the fun and none of the stress!

▶

What about asking The Parents if you can have just one friend stay over? Then invite one of your quiet, well-behaved friends for the night (someone nice like me, and not loud like Bubble!). See if that changes their minds about letting you have a few of your friends over.

letter 2

Scary sleepover

Dear Best Friends,
One of my friends, Lizzy, has invited me to her house for a Halloween sleepover. The thing is, she says we're going to do a seance, and I'm really scared. What should I do?

Laura, 12, Bridgeport

 Just tell her you can't make it. You won't be missing anything because scaring yourself stupid is not much fun. Besides, I'm sure you can find somewhere else to go for a laugh on Halloween.

 Talk to the other girls who were invited — I bet some of them feel the same as you. Then all of you tell her you'd love to come to her sleepover, but not if she's going to do scary stuff like that.

letter 3

Go away, Mom!

Dear Best Friends,
My problem's my mom. I really love her and everything, and all my friends think she's great — it's just that she hangs around all the time. If I have someone over she makes a big fuss. "Do they want a drink?", "Are they hungry?" etc. — and if we're up in my room, she'll come in and join the conversation and stuff! Now she wants to have a sleepover for my eleventh birthday, and I'm kind of dreading it. What should I do?

May, 10, Boulder

Hmmm. The thing with having a hovering mom is that having friends who think she's great just makes it worse! The thing to do is to sit down with her and talk about this, but DON'T go telling her to buzz off (I mean, how would you feel if someone told you that, or if your mom took no notice of you?). Instead, talk about planning your sleepover together and ask her to take care of the food while you handle the games. Then tell her you'll be playing "Truth or Dare" up in your room from 10 pm and that you'd like it to be strictly out of bounds for parents. I'm sure she'll understand and, because you've included her in the fun, she won't be offended.

Your mom sounds lovely! Let her help you out!

Molly's right. You need to include her a little, or get a new mom!

letter 4

No friends!

Dear Best Friends,

My name is Amy and I've just moved here from Memphis. I've been at my new school for two weeks now but haven't made any friends yet. My mom suggested a sleepover. What do you think?

Amy, 11, Paducah

What the Best Friends say

Whoa, Amy! Sleepovers are great fun with friends but not so easy with people you hardly know. That's way too much pressure — you'd be worrying about whether they're happy and what they think of you all night long. And what if there were an argument or it turned out that you didn't get along with one of the girls? A sleepover is too much to take on too soon.

Aw, Amy, it's awful being the new girl, isn't it? But don't worry, you will make friends soon. I think it would be much better if you tried to join in what some of the other girls are doing. Ask one of the girls what she's doing on the weekend — see if she gets the hint and invites you along. And what about after-school stuff, like a drama group or a dance class? They're great ways to meet new friends.

Teddy bear or no teddy bear?
I always sleep with my teddy bear, Mr. Pooh. Should I take him with me to my friend Tiffany's sleepover next week?

Mr. Pooh's slightly embarrassed owner, 10, Peoria

 I know loads of girls who have stuffed toys! They can be especially comforting if you're in a strange house. I always take Bearino to the BFs' sleepovers, but I just slip him out of my bag and under the blanket with me so no one sees him.

 Or maybe it's time to get used to leaving your teddy bear home — try going without him for this one night and see how you feel. You might surprise yourself! (And remember, he'll be there when you get home!)

letter 6

Best friend stress
Dear Best Friends,
Help! I'm having a sleepover on my birthday next month, but the problem is my best friend, Sally. She's great fun but she can be a little wild. She always wants to do stuff like make prank phone calls and sneak out of the house, and I'm getting really stressed that my parents are going to freak. I've asked her to promise not to do stuff, but she just laughs and calls me boring.

Anxious 12-year-old, Springfield

Your friend Sally sounds like our Bubble! What we do with Bubble when she's on one of her "missions" is to change her direction by saying, "Hey, isn't it pizza time?" or by putting on one of her CDs really loudly. Just prepare yourself with some of the Best Friends' alternative entertainment ideas from the last chapter (Page 68).

At the risk of sounding like a baby, what about talking to your mom first? I'm sure she would be happy to take the blame for being the "party pooper" by making her house rules clear to your guests (see parents' tips on page 13) and secretly monitoring the front door and telephone for "illegal" use. Your friend never has to know you've snitched on her!

letter 7

The 'B' word

Dear Best Friends,
Is it ever OK to invite boys to a sleepover?

Debbie, 12, Helena

What the Best Friends say

No waaaayyy! Next!

I agree with Missy. This is strictly a girl event. My brother (the ever-annoying Billy) is always busting in when I've got my girlfriends over "for a laugh," and it always causes much screaming and uproar. Girls simply do not want boys in their bedroom. Fact!

letter 8

Party pickle

Dear Best Friends,
My name is Lily. I've got a little problem with the sleepover I'm having next month. I'm only allowed to invite three girls, but there are six of us who hang around together. I don't want to hurt anyone's feelings. What should I do?

Lily, 11, San Diego

Invite the three girls you get along with best and explain separately to the other three that you'd love to invite them but numbers were strictly limited. As they say, you can't please all of the people all of the time.

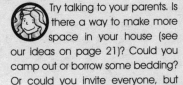 Try talking to your parents. Is there a way to make more space in your house (see our ideas on page 21)? Could you camp out or borrow some bedding? Or could you invite everyone, but only have a few girls stay overnight?

letter 9

Hanger on

Dear Best Friends,

My little sister who's six is really annoying. Whenever I have a sleepover, she always hangs around, following us and being a pain in the neck. Help!

Angela, 10, Tulsa

 Ship her out to the grandparents for the night but make it like she's getting a special treat. Give her something you know she'd like — your fave hair clip, a new coloring book — to take with her for being a good girl.

I've mentioned my twin Billy, haven't I? Mom knows how much he winds up me and the Friends, so she either tries to get him to stay the night at one of his pals', or she gets Dad to take him to the movies. Either that or I bribe him to stay away. A bag of tortilla chips usually buys me about an hour of peace.

 Aw, she's only little and trying to be like you! Be patient and tell her she can sit and watch but not interfere — just think how happy you'll make her.

Spooked out

Dear Best Friends,
I was at a friend's sleepover the other night when she got out a scary movie. I tried to say I didn't want to see it, but I was the only one, so I ended up watching it. I'm still having nightmares now. What would the Friends have done?

Spooked, 11, Louisville

 Well, first off, I think you need to do something about those nightmares. Tell your mom and dad what happened, let them know how upset you are, and I'm sure they can help you. If you don't want to tell them, what about a school counselor or friendly teacher? And remember, scary films are not real!

This is a tough one. I would've said watching the film would get me in real trouble if my parents found out, and since the movie was sure to spook me, and I would probably have nightmares, it was pretty certain my parents would find out. So I'd have to insist we didn't watch it. If my "friend" put it on anyway, I'd call my parents and ask them to pick me up. I know it sounds a little extreme, but if someone tries to make you do something that will clearly upset you, then they're not that great a friend.

Girl trouble

Dear Best Friends,
My problem is that my two best friends, Jenny and Rachel, are always arguing. They never agree on anything! And at Jenny's last sleepover, they had a major argument and both ended up pouting for most of the night. Now I'm planning a sleepover and I'm worried that the same thing's going to happen. Any suggestions?

Sam, 12, New Orleans

Before your sleepover, speak to the two girls separately about your worries and ask them, as a favor to you, not to argue. If they do start arguing, stand between them, ask them to calm down, and give each girl a minute or two to make her point, while the other girl *must* be quiet and listen. You must be relaxed, firm, and strong. When both girls have had their say, offer a solution to the argument without taking sides.

Get them to have a fight! Seriously! One time Missy and I had an argument that we settled by having a silly-string fight (see page 92). It was so crazy, we just cracked up laughing and forgot all about our stupid fight.

letter 12

A special something
Dear Best Friends,
I'm planning my first major sleepover. I want it to be really special but can't think what to do. Any suggestions?

Jess, 11, Minneapolis

Yeah! Do the cool quiz in the next exciting chapter!

The Quiz

What kind of hostess are you? Which is the theme for you? Can you handle party-prep stress? Do you make a good guest? Find out with our very revealing quiz!

Best Friends TOP TIP For a laugh, try out our quiz on your friends on the night of your sleepover, after lights-out. Just remember to put this book, a pencil, and a flashlight by your bed, and quiz away into the small hours!

What kind of sleepover queen R U?

Check off one of the answers after each question, then turn to page 111, add up your scores, and find your hostess profile. And, please note, we only accept honest answers here, Friend!

1 When was the last time you had friends (more than one) over to your house?
a) Within the last few days
b) About a week or so ago
c) Over a month ago
d) Over two weeks ago
e) Last weekend

2 Which word best describes you? (If you can't decide or are too bashful, ask a friend which one she thinks best suits you!)

a) Funny
b) Chatty
c) Caring
d) Cool
e) Rowdy

3 When it comes to letting you have parties, what would best describe your parents' attitude?

a) They just let us go ahead and do it.

b) They have a whole list of rules, which they constantly talk about.

c) Mom gets really excited — helping with the decorations and stuff — and Dad is pretty relaxed, making himself useful with little odd jobs.

d) They're OK if there are just a few of us, but if things get loud they get a little tense.

e) They're enthusiastic, which is great, but when they try to join in, it can get a little awkward!

4 Your idea of a good time with your friends is:

a) Eating pizzas and slurping cola

b) Staying up late, watching videos

c) Hanging out, making up games and winning prizes

d) Having a really good gossip session

e) Having a luxurious pampering session

5 Which of the following places and time periods would you most enjoy?

a) London in the groovy 1960s — all those fab clothes and wild parties with amazing celebrities

b) The next century — when we each have our own spaceship parked in the driveway and fly off to a theme-park planet for fun!

c) The nineteenth century in the Wild West — riding horses around amazing scenery all day and looking totally cool

d) Egypt a couple of thousand years back — making like Queen Cleopatra, being pampered all day, and living in incredible palaces

e) Some time when there's no hunger and no wars going on

6 You are holding a karaoke competition and you fail to win first prize. What's your reaction?

a) Oh, sure, like I'd be bothered by *that*

b) A little down; I know I sing really well

c) Start the next game as soon as possible

d) Be really happy for the person who won

e) Feel slightly disappointed, but happy for the winner

7 Which of these statements best describes your sleeping habits?

a) I like to stay up late but get a little groggy if I don't get a good ten hours' sleep.

b) I sometimes find it hard to go to sleep.

c) I love to sleep, and nod off really easily.

d) I often stay awake half the night!

e) I usually like to sleep in, especially on weekends.

8 You're having a sleepover, and two of your friends start having a big argument about something. Things are getting heated up. What do you do?

a) Try to settle it by offering my opinion on whatever they're arguing about

b) Stay calm and try to guide their argument toward an agreement

c) Let them argue it out

d) Try to distract them by starting a fun game

e) Tell both parties how much they are stressing me out, and ask them to stop. Now!

9 Do you worry about what other people think about you and where you live?
a) If I'm honest, yes, quite a lot
b) Fairly often — it's nice to be liked!
c) Very rarely
d) Not when they're good friends
e) Never

10 Which of these most accurately describes the current condition of your bedroom?
a) A cool hangout, with the focus on my TV and stereo
b) Hmmm . . . I've been meaning to tidy it up for a few days now — so it's a little messy, with my homework scattered around and my stinky sneakers in the corner. Otherwise it's pretty average: posters, bed, computer, etc.
c) Stylish, with a makeup table full of interesting clutter and a closet crammed with clothes
d) An adult-free zone, littered with lots of crazy stuff, loads of posters on the walls — and a few piles of clothes here and there

e) Cozy and relaxing — lots of stuffed teddy bears on the bed, interesting knickknacks everywhere

Now work out your scores!

Question 1	a = 1	b = 4	c =5	d = 2	e = 3
Question 2	a = 4	b = 1	c = 2	d = 3	e = 5
Question 3	a = 3	b = 5	c = 1	d = 2	e = 4
Question 4	a = 5	b = 3	c = 4	d = 1	e = 2
Question 5	a = 1	b = 3	c = 5	d = 2	e = 4
Question 6	a = 3	b = 1	c = 5	d = 2	e = 4
Question 7	a = 4	b = 5	c = 2	d = 3	e = 1
Question 8	a = 5	b = 2	c = 3	d = 4	e = 1
Question 9	a = 1	b = 2	c = 3	d = 4	e = 5
Question 10	a = 3	b = 4	c = 1	d = 5	e = 2

If you scored under 18: Ooh-la-la lady!

Ups: You are mature, super confident, and pride yourself on having good taste in all things. You also have the potential to be one of the best sleepover hostesses ever!

Downs: Although you are hugely talented, you can be a little too competitive — try to let your guests share some of the limelight!

You are most like: Princess
Recommended theme:
Glittery disco
Top activities: Karaoke
competitions and late-
night gossiping

If you scored 18–25: Laid-back gal!

Ups: You are enthusiastic, love to have fun, are truly giving, and like nothing better than to be part of a happy group of friends. You are a very kind and generous host.

Downs: You can be a little wimpy at times, but if you want your sleepover to run smoothly, you have to learn to take charge and make things happen yourself.

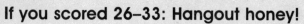

You are most like: Flower
Recommended theme:
Exotic East
Top activities: Giant sundae-
making, pampering, and
makeovers

If you scored 26–33: Hangout honey!

Ups: Everyone wants to come to your place because,

besides being super trendy, you are also very loyal to your friends, love a laugh, are totally honest and intelligent, and make a mega-chilled hostess.

Downs: Sometimes you can be a little too cool and, because you have everyone over so often, you don't always make a big effort as a hostess. Try to do something sort of different each time you entertain, and make sure you always find time to talk to each guest individually to let her know you appreciate her being there.

You are most like: Missy

Recommended theme:
Hollywood glamor

Top activities: Checking out the latest movies and late-night pranks

If you scored 34–41: The giggler

Ups: You adore your friends, love acting silly, are witty and wise, and make a natural leader. You are a confident and very capable hostess.

Downs: You try so hard to get everything right that you sometimes forget to have fun. So what if no one wants to do something you've planned? And what's the big deal if your mom gets involved? Stop being a control freak and go with the flow!

You are most like: Molly

Recommended theme:
None (you don't have to *have* one, y'know!)

Top activities: Making yummy snacks and playing late-night "Truth or Dare"

If you scored over 41: Ms. Va-Va-Voom!

Ups: Slightly crazy, full of life, very excitable, and exciting to be around — that's you! Plus you make a great guest — always enthusiastic and always spreading good vibes.

Downs: Your scatterbrain nature (and possibly your worrywart parents) have made your hosting skills somewhat, uhm, basic. You need to calm down and think about what your guests might want to do, rather than rushing around like crazy.

You are most like: Bubble

Recommended theme: Cowboy campout

Top activities: Pizza-making and chilling out watching a late-night movie

Almost good-bye!

The time has come, Best Friend, for you to try the sleepover world by yourself (sob!). And, y'know, I'm confident that you are going to make a totally happening sleepover hostess. BUT, before we go, the other BFs and I thought that we should mention a few of our fave things to do with girlfriends when we're not having sleepovers. So, seekers of fun, read on and get ready for more girlfriend gatherings. . . .

Some Other Get-Together Ideas

"This sounds impressive! Have *we* done all these?"

"You bet we have!"

"I think it would be fun if every Friend's ambition was to do at least, like, ten of them before teenagedom strikes!"

Good idea, Princess! OK, Friend, if you want to try it, just check off each girly gathering as you finish it. When you've scored a magical ten, that means you've racked up ten magical memories that you and your pals will share forever and ever!

"Way to go, Moll!"

OK, let's get started!

☐ Have a bad hair day— on purpose!

Meet in a friend's bedroom and give yourselves the freakiest hairstyles you can. For a spiky, bush effect, spray on lots of hairspray and then backcomb (or "tease" — with a comb, make small movements from the tips down to the roots). Then, for extra punkdom, add some temporary-color spray (available very cheaply from larger drugstores), feathers, cheapo tiaras, and whatever else you like.

☐ Be ice fairies at the skating rink

Go to your nearest ice skating rink (check on the Internet or in the phone book to find one) and skate around in a blur of elegance and furry earmuffs.

Best Friends TOP TIP

When you first get on the ice, marching along in little baby steps will help you to find your balance. Then work up a little speed, add a glide and, before you know it, you're doing it!

❑ Score at the bowling alley

Going bowling is great fun, not that expensive, and really easy to learn.

❑ Eat sweets and cry!

There's no better way to cheer up an unhappy friend than a bunch of girls getting together and indulging in a little chocolate therapy — then talking about your problems.

❝For supreme chocolatey comfort, top off a mug of hot chocolate with a handful of mini marshmallows and whipped cream — who could stay sad with that in their hands?!❞

❑ Be backyard beach babes

Let the beach come to you and your friends on a sunny day. Put on your swimsuit and shades, grab the sunscreen and a big bunch of glossy magazines, and lounge around your little sister's wading pool (well, a girl needs someplace to cool her tootsies).

❝For the ultimate in sun-chick sophistication, sip one of my smoothies (see page 54) poured over ice in a tall glass.**❞**

❑ Head for the fearground! Uh, sorry, fairground

Ask a parent to take you and your girlfriends to a theme park, vote on which of the scary big rides you all dare to go on — then get ready to SCRRREEEEAAMMM!!!! as you hurtle toward Jupiter at a gazillion miles an hour.

★ Best Friends **TOP TIP** ★

Save the hot dogs and cotton candy for after the ride...your tummy will thank you!

❑ Create a fashion-design studio

Get all your friends to bring a bunch of old clothes — especially jeans and other denim stuff — and loads of sewing materials (scissors, threads, patches, sequins, fake gemstones, fabric paint and glue, etc.) and hole up in a bedroom for an evening designing one outfit each.

*“Go crazy ripping —
the distressed look is sooo
in!”*

☐ Pretend you're a new pop act

Get a copy of the lyrics of a catchy song by a new girl band (some of the CDs come with lyrics; otherwise, check out the teen magazines) and get together with your friends to learn your parts. Then, you'll be ready to burst into "spontaneous" renditions of your "hit" at the drop of a hat.

Best Friends TOP TIP

You could also say stuff like, "Ooh, I've had enough of rehearsals today" and "I hope no one recognizes us."

☐ Make like a cool skateboard park punk

Transform yourselves into "skateheads" by pushing your jeans down to hip level (while pulling your underpants upward, so the tops are showing), putting on your baggiest T-shirt, scruffiest sneakers, and backward baseball cap, then heading off to the park.

❏ The pizza pilgrimage

There are times in every girl's life when all she needs is a pizza place and the company of good friends to be in absolute heaven.

"Everyone agree to get really glammed-up for your trip out — it'll make it much more special.**"**

❏ Be a cyber clan

Arrange to instant message each other on a certain day at a certain time. Before you go online, make up cyber aliases for yourselves and invent some kind of secret code that only you know.

"Here's some text slang we Friends use:**"**

BCNU	– be seeing you
ESOSL	– endless snorts of stupid laughter
GG	– gotta go
HHOJ	– ha ha only joking
L8R	– later!
GF	– girlfriend!
ZAM	– zzz's are me (i.e., bedtime!)
ZZZOVA	– sleepover!

❏ Make up your own cheerleader routine

Get together to learn the following basic moves and then add a few high kicks, jumps, and a chant.

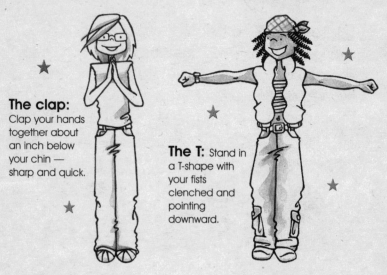

The clap:
Clap your hands together about an inch below your chin — sharp and quick.

The T: Stand in a T-shape with your fists clenched and pointing downward.

The goalpost:
Stand with your arms raised straight up, touching the sides of your head and clenching your fists.

Cone head:
From the goalpost position, unclench your fists and clap your hands together.

High V: From the goalpost position, widen your arms so your body forms a V.

Low V: This time, for an upside-down V, move your arms straight down by your sides.

The chant: The idea is to get the crowd cheering with you. Try the traditional ones like: "Give me a C (crowd: C!). Give me an O (crowd: O!). Give me another O (crowd: O!). Give me an L (crowd: L!). Whaddya got? (Crowd: COOL!!!!!)." You start wildly jumping around at this point.

66 Add to your bag of tricks by watching your school's cheerleaders and copying their moves. Before you know it, you and your friends will be ready to take your show on the road — best of all, it's FUN. **99**

❏ Shop! Shop! Shop!

Is there a better place for a girl to be than in a dressing room on a Saturday afternoon, with a few dollars in her pocket, trying on some of the trendiest clothes around, and a bunch of her giggling best friends telling her that she looks simply divine? No. There is not!

❝Don't forget the joy of the mini shopping trip. Even if you're short on cash, finding the best bargain on a beaded choker can still be a truly uplifting mission.❞

❏ Go sports wild followed by a pig-out picnic

Summery kinda day? Grab a bat, ball, and plenty of munchies, and head for the park! Try a game of softball or, if there aren't that many of you, throw a frisbee around.

Frustrated? Annoyed? Parents on your case? Schoolwork getting you down? Let it all out by hitting that ball just as hard as you can, Friend!

❏ Watch some big-screen action

It's gotta be a mega blockbuster, with eardrum-rattling stereo surround-sound, a humongous box of popcorn, giant cup of slurpy drink and, of course, your best friends at your side. It'll rock you to another planet and back, and leave you totally inspired and refreshed!

❝ Head for a sit-down eatery later — essential for a good chat about what you all thought about the film. **❞**

We really are going this time...

And so, with a big lump in our throats, we Best Friends must say good-bye to you, our newest Friend... but only for now, because we've got loads more to share with you.

So see you soon, we hope.
Lots of hugs, ★

Molly
x

Later, Missy ☺

Just remember,
you are the best!
Princess xx

★

We'll be
thinking of ya!!
Flower xxxx

★

And, hey, hope you have the best
sleepovers ever! Bubble! ooo

★